REFLECTIONS
FOR
ADVENT

27 November – 23 December 2017

CHRISTOPHER COCKSWORTH
MALCOLM GUITE
PAULA GOODER

with an introduction to Advent
by MARGARET WHIPP

Church House Publishing
Church House
Great Smith Street
London SW1P 3AZ

ISBN 978 1 78140 024 1

Published 2017 by Church House Publishing
Copyright © The Archbishops' Council 2017

The opinions expressed in this book are those of the
authors and do not necessarily reflect the official policy
of the General Synod or The Archbishops' Council of the
Church of England.

Liturgical editor: Peter Moger
Series editor: Hugh Hillyard-Parker
Designed and typeset by Hugh Hillyard-Parker
Copy edited by: Ros Connelly
Printed by CPI Group (UK) Ltd, Croydon, CR0 4YY

What do you think of *Reflections for Daily Prayer*?

We'd love to hear from you – simply email us at

publishing@churchofengland.org

or write to us at

Church House Publishing, Church House,
Great Smith Street, London SW1P 3AZ.

Visit **www.dailyprayer.org.uk** for more
information on the *Reflections* series, ordering
and subscriptions.

Contents

About *Reflections for Advent*

Based on the *Common Worship Lectionary* readings for Morning Prayer, these daily reflections are designed to refresh and inspire times of personal prayer. The aim is to provide rich, contemporary and engaging insights into Scripture.

Each page lists the Lectionary readings for the day, with the main psalms for that day highlighted in **bold**. The Collect of the day – either the *Common Worship* collect or the shorter additional Collect – is also included.

For those using this book in conjunction with a service of Morning Prayer, the following conventions apply: a psalm printed in parentheses is omitted if it has been used as the opening canticle at that office; a psalm marked with an asterisk may be shortened if desired.

A short reflection is provided on either the Old or New Testament reading. Popular writers, experienced ministers, biblical scholars and theologians have contributed to this series, bringing their own emphases, enthusiasms and approaches to biblical interpretation to bear.

Regular users of Morning Prayer and *Time to Pray* (from *Common Worship: Daily Prayer*) and anyone who follows the Lectionary for their regular Bible reading will benefit from the rich variety of traditions represented in these stimulating and accessible pieces.

This volume also includes both a simple form of *Common Worship: Morning Prayer* (see pp. 34–5) and a short form of Night Prayer – also known as Compline – (see pp. 38–41), particularly for the benefit of those readers who are new to the habit of the Daily Office or for any reader while travelling.

About the authors

Christopher Cocksworth is the Bishop of Coventry. He read Theology at the University of Manchester. After teaching in secondary education, he trained for ordination and pursued doctoral studies, serving in parochial and chaplaincy ministry and in theological education, latterly as Principal of Ridley Hall, Cambridge.

Stephen Cottrell is the Bishop of Chelmsford. Before this he was Bishop of Reading and has worked in parishes in London, Chichester, and Huddersfield and as Pastor of Peterborough Cathedral. He is a well-known writer and speaker on evangelism, spirituality and catechesis. His best-selling *How to Pray* (CHP) and *How to Live* (CHP) have recently been reissued.

Paula Gooder is Theologian in Residence for the Bible Society. She is a writer and lecturer in biblical studies, author of a number of books including *Journey to the Empty Tomb, The Meaning is in the Waiting* and *Heaven*, and a co-author of the *Pilgrim* course. She is also a Reader in the Church of England.

Malcolm Guite is the Chaplain of Girton College, Cambridge, a poet and author of *What do Christians Believe?; Faith, Hope and Poetry; Sounding the Seasons: Seventy Sonnets for the Christian Year; The Singing Bowl; Word in the Wilderness* and *Mariner: A voyage with Samuel Taylor Coleridge.*

Rachel Treweek is the Bishop of Gloucester and the first female diocesan bishop in England. She served in two parishes in London and was Archdeacon of Northolt and later Hackney. Prior to ordination she was a speech and language therapist and is a trained practitioner in conflict transformation.

Margaret Whipp is the Lead Chaplain for the Oxford University Hospitals. Her first profession was in medicine. Since ordination she has served in parish ministry, university chaplaincy, and most recently as Senior Tutor at Ripon College Cuddesdon. She writes and researches in pastoral theology, enjoys singing and long-distance pilgrimage trails, and is an Honorary Canon of Christ Church Cathedral, Oxford.

Counting the days
– A reflection on the season of Advent

An old friend recently posted a photograph of her newborn baby. He was utterly delightful, a real sweetheart, dressed in a cosy blue bodysuit with the caption across his chest: 'I've just done nine months inside.'

A baby's time from conception to birth averages 40 weeks. In that time, there is a huge amount of anatomical and physiological change, emotional and social adjustment. The slow, gradual ripening of a pregnancy proceeds at a pace that cannot be hurried. Our human gestation period of nine months is as nothing, though, compared to the time taken by other large mammals: horses take eleven months, rhinos 14 months, sperm whales 16 months, elephants famously take 22 months, while – top of the league – frilled sharks carry their young for up to three and a half years.

While each expectant mother counts the days, the seed within her womb is growing and developing its own distinctive vitality. There is a necessary sequence to its embryonic development, laid down through long ages of genetic and evolutionary wisdom. The patience of growing things rests in following this steady course of developmental progress, through which there can be no skipping of the intermediate stages. As she counts each passing day, the mother trusts and prays that her precious seed of new life, hidden deep within the womb, will slowly unfold to be a healthy and happy child. Gestation is so much a matter of patience and time.

'Above all, trust in the slow work of God,' counselled the Jesuit priest Teilhard de Chardin in one of his wartime letters. He was writing from the muddy quagmire of the trenches to a young cousin, Marguerite, who was struggling to find her way forward in life. Teilhard's advice is as relevant to expectant parents as it is to pastors and politicians, researchers and creative artists, or to young people in search of their vocation. 'We are, quite naturally, impatient in everything to reach the end without delay.' It is hard to live in the liminal space, to be in formation, en route to something unknown, something new. 'And yet it is the law of all progress that it is made by passing through some stages of instability – and that may take a very long time'.

Some of the most important things in life take a long time to ripen to maturity. Giving the necessary time to nourish our own souls, to nurture the mental and spiritual resources of others, to incubate the germ of an idea, these are the motherly tasks of many a season of pregnant waiting. Things must unfold and develop, slowly quickening and coming to birth, in their own good time. Our task, like that of a farmer, is to feed and water, and patiently tend, whatever seeds of hope God has planted for an unknown, and unimaginable future.

The season of Advent, with all its 'earnest looking forward', invites us to count the days in a spirit of watchful waiting. Against the restless busyness of the world around, Christians have good reason to slow down, to embrace a holy patience, to cherish with quiet expectancy the sweetest grace that God is bringing to birth.

Margaret Whipp

Adapted from *The Grace of Waiting*,
Norwich: Canterbury Press, 2017.

Building daily prayer into daily life

In our morning routines there are many tasks we do without giving much thought to them, and others that we do with careful attention. Daily prayer and Bible reading is a strange mixture of these. These are disciplines (and gifts) that we as Christians should have in our daily pattern, but they are not tasks to be ticked off. Rather they are a key component of our developing relationship with God. In them is *life* – for the fruits of this time are to be lived out by us – and to be most fruitful, the task requires both purpose and letting go.

In saying a daily office of prayer, we make the deliberate decision to say 'yes' to spending time with God – the God who is always with us. In prayer and attentive reading of the Scriptures, there is both a conscious entering into God's presence and a 'letting go' of all we strive to control: both are our acknowledgement that it is God who is God.

> *… come before his presence with a song…*
>
> *Know that the Lord is God;*
> *it is he that has made us and we are his;*
> *we are his people and the sheep of his pasture.*
>
> *Enter his gates with thanksgiving…*
>
> *(Psalm 100, a traditional Canticle at Morning Prayer)*

If we want a relationship with someone to deepen and grow, we need to spend time with that person. It can be no surprise that the same is true between us and God.

In our daily routines, I suspect that most of us intentionally look in the mirror; occasionally we might see beyond the surface of our external reflection and catch a glimpse of who we truly are. For me, a regular pattern of daily prayer and Bible reading is like a hard look in a clean mirror: it gives a clear reflection of myself, my life and the world in which I live. But it is more than that, for in it I can also see the reflection of God who is most clearly revealed in Jesus Christ and present with us now in the Holy Spirit.

This commitment to daily prayer is about our relationship with the God who is love. St Paul, in his great passage about love, speaks of now seeing 'in a mirror, dimly' but one day seeing face to face: 'Now I know only in part; then I will know fully, even as I have been fully known' (1 Corinthians 13.12). Our daily prayer is part of that seeing in a mirror dimly, and it is also part of our deep yearning for an ever-clearer vision of our God. As we read Scripture, the past and the future converge in the present moment. We hear words from long ago – some of which can appear strange and confusing – and yet, the Holy Spirit is living and active in the present. In this place of relationship and revelation, we open ourselves to the possibility of being changed, of being reshaped in a way that is good for us and all creation.

It is important that the words of prayer and scripture should penetrate deep within rather than be a mere veneer. A quiet location is therefore a helpful starting point. For some, domestic circumstances or daily schedule make that difficult, but it is never impossible to become more fully present to God. The depths of our being can still be accessed no matter the world's clamour and activity. An awareness of this is all part of our journey from a false sense of control to a place of letting go, to a place where there is an opportunity for transformation.

Sometimes in our attention to Scripture there will be connection with places of joy or pain; we might be encouraged or provoked or both. As we look and see and encounter God more deeply, there will be thanksgiving and repentance; the cries of our heart will surface as we acknowledge our needs and desires for ourselves and the world. The liturgy of Morning Prayer gives this voice and space.

I find it helpful to begin Morning Prayer by lighting a candle. This marks my sense of purpose and my acknowledgement of Christ's presence with me. It is also a silent prayer for illumination as I prepare to be attentive to what I see in the mirror, both of myself and of God. Amid the revelation of Scripture and the cries of my heart, the constancy of the tiny flame bears witness to the hope and light of Christ in all that is and will be.

When the candle is extinguished, I try to be still as I watch the smoke disappear. For me, it is symbolic of my prayers merging with the day. I know that my prayer and the reading of Scripture are not the smoke and mirrors of delusion. Rather, they are about encounter and discovery as I seek to venture into the day to love and serve the Lord as a disciple of Jesus Christ.

+*Rachel Treweek*

Lectio Divina – a way of reading the Bible

Lectio Divina is a contemplative way of reading the Bible. It dates back to the early centuries of the Christian Church and was established as a monastic practice by Benedict in the sixth century. It is a way of praying the Scriptures that leads us deeper into God's word. We slow down. We read a short passage more than once. We chew it over slowly and carefully. We savour it. Scripture begins to speak to us in a new way. It speaks to us personally, and aids that union we have with God through Christ, who is himself the Living Word.

Make sure you are sitting comfortably. Breathe slowly and deeply. Ask God to speak to you through the passage that you are about to read.

This way of praying starts with our silence. We often make the mistake of thinking prayer is about what we say to God. It is actually the other way round. God wants to speak to us. He will do this through the Scriptures. So don't worry about what to say. Don't worry if nothing jumps out at you at first. God is patient. He will wait for the opportunity to get in. He will give you a word and lead you to understand its meaning for you today.

First reading: Listen

As you read the passage listen for a word or phrase that attracts you. Allow it to arise from the passage as if it is God's word for you today. Sit in silence repeating the word or phrase in your head.

Then say the word or phrase aloud.

Second reading: Ponder

As you read the passage again, ask how this word or phrase speaks to your life and why it has connected with you. Ponder it carefully. Don't worry if you get distracted – it may be part of your response to offer to God. Sit in silence and then frame a single sentence that begins to say aloud what this word or phrase says to you.

Third reading: Pray

As you read the passage for the last time, ask what Christ is calling from you. What is it that you need to do or consider or relinquish or take on as a result of what God is saying to you in this word or phrase? In the silence that follows the reading, pray for the grace of the Spirit to plant this word in your heart.

If you are in a group, talk for a few minutes and pray with each other.

If you are on your own, speak your prayer to God either aloud or in the silence of your heart.

If there is time, you may even want to read the passage a fourth time, and then end with the same silence before God with which you began.

+Stephen Cottrell

Monday 27 November

Psalms 92, **96** *or* **71**
Isaiah 14.3-20
Matthew 9.18-34

Matthew 9.18-34

'If I only touch his cloak' (v.21)

In Matthew 9 we find a string of stories in which people with great need encounter Jesus: first there is the story of the raising of Jairus' daughter, which is wrapped around the story of the healing of the woman with a haemorrhage; then comes the healing of two blind men and finally that of a person, possessed by a demon, who was mute.

In contrast to the various interest groups that Jesus had encountered in his ministry so far, who all in their different ways had much to lose, each one of these people (or those who petitioned Jesus on their behalf) were aware of a great and gaping need: a child at the point of death; a woman outcast from society by her uncleanness; and men who experienced daily exclusion because they could not see or speak. It was this need that drove Jairus to abandon his dignity and kneel before Jesus in the street, or drove the woman with a haemorrhage to risk the wrath of the crowd when she made them unclean by brushing against them.

Matthew 5.3 is sometimes translated (e.g. New English Bible) as 'blessed are those who know their need of God'. This is a powerful translation and puts in a nutshell the essence of the nature of Jesus' good news. It is only good news if, like the people in this passage, you know you really need it.

COLLECT

Eternal Father,
whose Son Jesus Christ ascended to the throne of heaven
    that he might rule over all things as Lord and King:
keep the Church in the unity of the Spirit
and in the bond of peace,
and bring the whole created order to worship at his feet;
who is alive and reigns with you,
in the unity of the Holy Spirit,
one God, now and for ever.

Reflection by **Paula Gooder**

Psalms **97**, 98, 100 *or* **73**   **Tuesday 28 November**
Isaiah 17
Matthew 9.35 – 10.15

Matthew 9.35 – 10.15

'... the good news of the kingdom' (9.35)

Why share the good news of Jesus Christ? Proclaiming the good news of the kingdom lies right at the heart of the Christian faith. Jesus proclaimed it himself (9.35) and sent the twelve disciples out to do the same (10.7). During 2000 years of Christian history the Church has continued to share this mission (with varying degrees of enthusiasm). What can often go wrong, however, is a poor communication of why we share the good news of the kingdom.

It can sometimes sound as though we do so in order to force our views on others; or because we fear that too few people currently come to our churches; or because we need some more money. This passage reminds us that none of these lies behind Jesus' sharing of the good news. Jesus said what he said and did what he did because he was so moved with compassion for those around him. They were so lost, so rootless and visionless – like sheep without a shepherd – harassed and helpless that he could do no other than seek to help them.

When a few verses later he sent out the Twelve, he sent them out to be similarly moved with compassion, and similarly to offer love and encouragement. Our calling to proclaim the good news of Jesus Christ requires the same of us: to be deeply moved with compassion for those we meet. Anything less than this fails to live up to his example.

God the Father,
help us to hear the call of Christ the King
and to follow in his service,
whose kingdom has no end;
for he reigns with you and the Holy Spirit,
one God, one glory.

COLLECT

Reflection by **Paula Gooder**   11

Wednesday 29 November

Psalms 110, 111, **112** *or* **77**
Isaiah 19
Matthew 10.16-33

Matthew 10.16-33

'... what you hear whispered, proclaim from the housetops' (v.27)

It is easy to slip into assuming that what happens to others can't happen to us. It is fascinating to watch the media in the days following tragedies, as they search frantically for explanations of why something happened. If they find one, we breathe a collective sigh of relief. If we can point to an explanation of why something happened, it becomes easier to believe it won't happen to us.

In Matthew 10.24-28, Jesus makes very clear that the disciples should not for a moment imagine that they will escape the abuse that he has received. He came full of compassion for those around him; he healed them; listened to them; proclaimed the good news of the kingdom and ultimately died for them – and they called him the devil ('Beelzebul' was a name used for the devil).

The disciples, Jesus declares, when faced with the same challenge will fare no better. If this is what happened to Jesus, the disciples can expect it to happen to them too. By extension, if it happens to the disciples, we can also expect to be treated in the same way.

The importance of this is that we should not allow fear of what *could* happen – what people might say or do – to constrict us. If they are going to act like this anyway, we might as well proclaim our good news from the rooftops and at the top of our lungs!

COLLECT

Eternal Father,
whose Son Jesus Christ ascended to the throne of heaven
    that he might rule over all things as Lord and King:
keep the Church in the unity of the Spirit
and in the bond of peace,
and bring the whole created order to worship at his feet;
who is alive and reigns with you,
in the unity of the Holy Spirit,
one God, now and for ever.

Reflection by **Paula Gooder**

Psalms 47, 147.1-12
Ezekiel 47.1-12
or Ecclesiasticus 14.20-end
John 12.20-32

Thursday 30 November
Andrew the Apostle

John 12.20-32

'Those who love their life lose it' (v.25)

One of the challenges of reading the Gospels is to try to read the riddles they contain with a continued freshness and openness. Possibly one of the most complex riddles in the whole of the New Testament (a riddle that occurs in a slightly different form in each of the Gospels) can be found here in John 12.25 – those who love their life (the Greek word here is *psuchē*) will lose it, and those who hate it will keep it for eternal life.

On this, St Andrew's day, we have to be careful to read this riddle cautiously and thoughtfully. There are times in Christian history when it has been read in a 'bring it on' kind of way – let martyrdom come as a sign of how much I hate my life. This must surely be the wrong reading of what Jesus was saying here. His message is much more subtle and much more riddle-like. If we dedicate our whole existence to defending our rights, to accumulating more wealth, to holding on to what we have, then the most likely outcome will be that we will destroy it (the word 'lose' here might be better rendered 'destroy'). It is only when we loosen our grip, when we turn our backs on what instinct tells us to preserve, that we discover that we have held onto what matters most.

This is a riddle that St Andrew undoubtedly understood.

Almighty God,
who gave such grace to your apostle Saint Andrew
that he readily obeyed the call of your Son Jesus Christ
and brought his brother with him:
call us by your holy word,
and give us grace to follow you without delay
and to tell the good news of your kingdom;
through Jesus Christ your Son our Lord,
who is alive and reigns with you,
in the unity of the Holy Spirit,
one God, now and for ever.

COLLECT

Reflection by **Paula Gooder**   13

Friday 1 December

Matthew 11.2-19

'We played the flute for you, and you did not dance' (v.17)

It is tempting to subtitle this passage: 'some people are never happy'. In it Jesus pinpoints with characteristically uncomfortable accuracy a human tendency that we must all recognize: that tendency to grumble and groan on the sidelines rather than to join in with joy and delight.

Jesus' comment about his generation being like children in a market place calling to each other (v.16) is thought by many scholars to be an allusion to the vision of hope in Zechariah 8.4-5 which presents a vision of the old and young alike being in the market square, the old with a staff to mark respect and the children playing together. In Matthew the children aren't playing; they are simply sitting there grumbling.

In other words, the day of rejoicing has come. John came to point the way to the glorious new future. Jesus, the Messiah, is here, but his generation, rather than getting up and celebrating, sat around complaining that others wouldn't do as they were told – wouldn't dance when the music played nor mourn when they wailed. Their reproach didn't end there: John was criticized for eating and drinking too little and Jesus for eating and drinking too much (vv.18-19).

It is all too easy to miss the good news of the kingdom, not because it is missing but because we are too busy carping and complaining to see it. Such attitudes are not restricted to Jesus' generation.

COLLECT

Eternal Father,
whose Son Jesus Christ ascended to the throne of heaven
    that he might rule over all things as Lord and King:
keep the Church in the unity of the Spirit
and in the bond of peace,
and bring the whole created order to worship at his feet;
who is alive and reigns with you,
in the unity of the Holy Spirit,
one God, now and for ever.

Reflection by **Paula Gooder**

Psalm **145** *or* **76**, 79
Isaiah 24
Matthew 11.20-end

Saturday 2 December

Matthew 11.20-end

'... you have hidden these things from the wise' (v.25)

A question that emerges time and time again in the Old Testament is where wisdom is to be found. It is a question that still resonates today. Where do we look for the kind of wisdom that provides real answers to life's questions? A wisdom that offers security in an anxious and turbulent world and rest for the soul?

The answer, of course, is in Jesus. It is not for nothing that Jesus' invitation to come to him to find rest is one of the most quoted of all of Jesus' sayings. Who among us could turn down the offer of rest for our souls? The warning that lurks within Jesus' words, however, is that we should accept such wisdom for what it is and not try and turn it into something that it is not. It is the kind of wisdom that makes more sense to children than to those that consider themselves already wise. It is the kind of wisdom that is easy to come by and light to follow.

It is a natural human instinct to assume that the more true something is, the more complicated it must be, and if it doesn't appear complicated enough, to make it so. Jesus' wisdom, however, is not complicated: we learn by being yoked to him like an ox in a plough team, following wherever he goes. It may not be complicated but, since following him involves taking up our crosses (Matthew 10.38), it will take everything we have.

God the Father,
help us to hear the call of Christ the King
and to follow in his service,
whose kingdom has no end;
for he reigns with you and the Holy Spirit,
one God, one glory.

COLLECT

Reflection by **Paula Gooder**   15

Monday 4 December

Psalms **50**, 54 *or* 1, 2, 3
Isaiah 25.1-9
Matthew 12.1-21

Matthew 12.1-21

'Something greater ...' (v.6)

It's little wonder that the Pharisees 'went out' and set about getting rid of him. Jesus had entered *their* synagogue – and on the *sabbath* – searching out someone on whom he could prove his point – that he, Jesus, was Lord of the sabbath.

Jesus' dangerously controversial claim was made worse by his defence of the law-breaking activity of his disciples. They were simply not permitted to reap and thresh on the sabbath, no matter how small-scale their actions or whatever their apparent hunger.

Yet even though the law was abundantly clear and the interpreters agreed on its meaning, perhaps the Pharisees could have tolerated a sensible discussion within the terms of rabbinic argument. What they couldn't bear was the blasphemous basis of Jesus' argument that with him something greater than David, the temple and the sabbath had come among them.

Controversy about such fundamental symbols of national identity and religious significance – matters on which ethnic survival and promised salvation were seen to depend – was bound to lead to confrontation, and worse was to come. Now, though, Jesus withdraws from the fray. He departs in order to define the sort of greatness to be found in him, and the way he will exercise it. Jesus is God's servant, the bearer of God's Spirit. He brings justice for the nations and he does so gently, neither breaking nor quenching but healing and giving hope. Hence our Advent cry: 'Amen. Come, Lord Jesus!'.

C O L L E C T

Almighty God,
give us grace to cast away the works of darkness
and to put on the armour of light,
now in the time of this mortal life,
in which your Son Jesus Christ came to us in great humility;
that on the last day,
when he shall come again in his glorious majesty
    to judge the living and the dead,
we may rise to the life immortal;
through him who is alive and reigns with you,
in the unity of the Holy Spirit,
one God, now and for ever.

| *Reflection by* **Christopher Cocksworth**

Psalms **80**, 82 *or* **5**, 6 (8)
Isaiah 26.1-13
Matthew 12.22-37

Tuesday 5 December

Matthew 12.22-37

'... then the kingdom of God has come to you' (v.28)

Yesterday's reading faced us with questions about Jesus' identity – could he really be greater than David, the temple and the sabbath? Today's reading takes us deeper into the identity of Jesus by forcing us to analyse the source of his activity. In so doing we face stark questions about our own identity, and where we stand in relation to the source of all that is good.

Jesus brings speech and sight to a man deprived of both – not through natural disease but by demonic power. On whose authority does Jesus act: the ruler of the demons or the God of Israel? Jesus is not shy of logical argument. It is nonsense, he says, for Satan to cast out Satan. In fact, his case rests on an even more reasoned argument. There is evidence that the strong man has been tied up and his house plundered because those once held in captivity – the blind and the mute among them – are now set free. You decide, he says: is this abundantly good work a sign of God at work among you, God's hand reaching out to heal you and lift you up, or is it the mark of evil in your midst? On your answer depends your destiny, eternally.

Yet to answer well, you will need more than reasoned argument and discerning observation. You will need the Son of David to open your eyes and reset your speech to see and to confess that the child of Mary is truly the Son of Man – and that the Son of Man really is Emmanuel: God with us.

Almighty God,
as your kingdom dawns,
turn us from the darkness of sin to the
light of holiness,
that we may be ready to meet you
in our Lord and Saviour, Jesus Christ.

COLLECT

Wednesday 6 December

Matthew 12.38-end

'Teacher, we wish to see a sign from you' (v.38)

If Jesus really was the Servant of the Lord, full of God's Spirit and, thereby, the promised Son of Man who is Lord of the sabbath, then it wasn't unreasonable for the religious authorities to ask for some sort of sign to back up these momentous claims. It wasn't that Jesus objected to the request for evidence of spiritual credibility. After all, the great figures of old – Moses, Gideon, Elijah among them – had been supported by signs that reinforced their words. It was just that he knew that the sort of indicators of God's blessing on his ministry – healings, exorcisms, even a stilled storm – that had been clearly evident would not convince those whose hearts were hard.

Another sign would come, though, greater even than the sign of Jonah because something greater than Jonah and all the prophets had come with Jesus. This is the sign that will bring deliverance from the strongest grip of the monster that stalks humanity, release from the inexorable clutch of death. It won't just cause life to return to how it was. It will recreate life, raising it into life with God, for ever.

Although even this greatest sign will be dismissed by the hard of heart, for the new community of Jesus – those who are truly his mother, brothers and sisters – it will be more than a sign. It will be the reality of resurrection life, the lived experience of the will of Jesus' Father.

Waiting for the light of the child in the manger through the darkness of Advent is like waiting in Lent for the brilliance of resurrection dawn after the shadow of the tomb, for the light of Christ is the light of life.

COLLECT

Almighty God,
give us grace to cast away the works of darkness
and to put on the armour of light,
now in the time of this mortal life,
in which your Son Jesus Christ came to us in great humility;
that on the last day,
when he shall come again in his glorious majesty
    to judge the living and the dead,
we may rise to the life immortal;
through him who is alive and reigns with you,
in the unity of the Holy Spirit,
one God, now and for ever.

Reflection by **Christopher Cocksworth**

Psalms **42**, 43 *or* 14, **15**, 16
Isaiah 28.14-end
Matthew 13.1-23

Thursday 7 December

Matthew 13.1-23

'... many prophets and righteous people longed to see what you see' (v.17)

'That same day', writes Matthew. He wants to underline the connection with what has just happened. Earlier in the day, Jesus had defined his family of disciples as those who do the will of his Father. They are the people who hear 'the word of the kingdom' and understand it sufficiently to know that it calls them to follow Jesus and live in his way. They have seen and heard the parable that is Jesus himself. They have perceived that in the hidden form of the carpenter's son, the Servant of the Lord – beloved of God in whom God is well pleased – has come to bring the reality of the kingdom of heaven to the peoples of the earth, and they have joined him in that new life.

Jesus, the parable of God's purposes, speaks of God's purposes in parables – stories and sayings that, like him, bear a deeper meaning than their surface shows. To those who have responded to 'the word of the kingdom', Jesus explains the meaning of his parables so that they become a commentary on the life of the kingdom. For those who still stand on the outside, the parables are more of a challenge. But it is one to which they can rise. Jesus' community is not a closed circle. It is always open to those who are ready to receive the seed of the kingdom and determined to let it grow deep within them, bearing the good fruit of God's will on earth as in heaven.

COLLECT

Almighty God,
as your kingdom dawns,
turn us from the darkness of sin to the
light of holiness,
that we may be ready to meet you
in our Lord and Saviour, Jesus Christ.

Reflection by **Christopher Cocksworth**

Friday 8 December

Psalms **25**, 26 *or* 17, **19**
Isaiah 29.1-14
Matthew 13.24-43

Matthew 13.24-43

'I will proclaim what has been hidden' (v.35)

Parables make known the word of the kingdom. They reveal God's ways in hidden form. We need to search for the word veiled in the story. At first elusive, it becomes clear – slowly but surely.

That's how the kingdom of heaven comes to earth – at first hidden, then, finally, abundantly clear. It's hidden in the smallness of the mustard seed, a tiny speck of life buried in a large field. It's hidden in a little lump of sourdough that's mixed with three measures – about sixty pounds – of flour. The generative capacities of the seed and the leaven are out of all proportion to their begetting form: shrub as large as a tree, enough bread to feed a village.

The Son of Man, who makes known what has been hidden since the foundation of the world, does so as the one hidden in the form of a servant, born, as we shall soon celebrate, in human likeness as the child of Mary. Christmas is the 'day of small things' (Zechariah 4.10), the day of a child born in obscurity. With all those who are truly wise, we will rejoice on that day with exceedingly great joy (Matthew 2.10), not only because we are overwhelmed by the humility of the hidden God, but also because we are humbled before the one who will come with the angels as the judge of the world. For then, as the hidden realities come fully to light, evil will be burnt away and the children of the kingdom will shine with their Father's glory.

COLLECT

Almighty God,
give us grace to cast away the works of darkness
and to put on the armour of light,
now in the time of this mortal life,
in which your Son Jesus Christ came to us in great humility;
that on the last day,
when he shall come again in his glorious majesty
    to judge the living and the dead,
we may rise to the life immortal;
through him who is alive and reigns with you,
in the unity of the Holy Spirit,
one God, now and for ever.

Reflection by **Christopher Cocksworth**

Psalms **9**, (10) *or* 20, 21, **23**
Isaiah 29.15-end
Matthew 13.44-end

Saturday 9 December

Matthew 13.44-end

'Where then did this man get all this?' (v.56)

Jesus, travelling through Galilee, arrives at his home town, Nazareth, and teaches in the synagogue where he had been such a familiar figure. Astonishment at his teaching was not unusual, but here it took a nasty turn. How could such wisdom and power come from one they had seen growing up with his brothers and sisters, and who had earned his living in his father's firm of local builders? They were scandalized, Matthew tells us: the very reaction that Jesus had warned against earlier when he set out his case to John the Baptist that he was, as John had dared to hope, 'the one who is to come' (Matthew 11.2-6).

Luke tells us more about the incident, how it led to a riot and came very close to a lynching. For all their apparent piety, the people of Jesus' home town who had gathered in the synagogue to hear God's word, missed the treasure in their midst, the pearl of greatest price that was being put in their hands. They proved the point of the parables that Jesus had been telling. Although the word of the kingdom is scattered with indiscriminate grace, not everyone who hears will believe. The eyes of some will remain closed.

Those who see that this wisdom and these deeds of power come from God will use all their strength to take hold of not only his words and works but Jesus himself, the Saviour of the world found in the son of the carpenter, once wrapped in swaddling clothes and laid in a manger.

Almighty God,
as your kingdom dawns,
turn us from the darkness of sin to the
light of holiness,
that we may be ready to meet you
in our Lord and Saviour, Jesus Christ.

COLLECT

Reflection by **Christopher Cocksworth** | 21

Monday 11 December

Matthew 14.1-12

'Herod wanted to put him to death' (v.5)

On first reading, this gory account of John the Baptist's illegal execution seems like a distraction from Matthew's carefully staged narrative of Jesus' ministry, with the unfolding of his works and the unveiling of his ministry. On closer inspection, though, Jesus is woven into the story at every point.

Jesus bookends this flashback to John's death. Herod hears reports about Jesus that worry him. Jesus is told of John's fate, and takes himself out of the limelight. The flashback itself foreshadows the fate of Jesus. As 'they did to him whatever they pleased', so they will do to Jesus (Matthew 17.12). The destructive cameo of Herod Antipas' household is the antithesis of the picture Matthew has been painting of the life of the kingdom of heaven and the Servant of the Lord who brings it.

Yes, Herod senses the spiritual in Jesus but he's overtaken by superstition. Herod has his eyes on a prize – he wants John dead – but it brings him grief, deeply disturbing his spirit. Herod feasts with his family and admirers, but their indulgence descends into hellish debauchery. The feast that Jesus is soon to share with thousands will open a window to heaven.

This tale of Herod's excess is a parable not of the kingdom of heaven but of the kingdom of the enemy, the evil one from whose clutches 'the one who is come' is determined to set us free. Like the parables that Jesus told, it invites us to weave our stories into Jesus' story and not another.

COLLECT

O Lord, raise up, we pray, your power
and come among us,
and with great might succour us;
that whereas, through our sins and wickedness
we are grievously hindered
in running the race that is set before us,
your bountiful grace and mercy
may speedily help and deliver us;
through Jesus Christ your Son our Lord,
to whom with you and the Holy Spirit,
be honour and glory, now and for ever.

| *Reflection by* **Christopher Cocksworth**

Psalms **56**, 57 *or* 32, **36**
Isaiah 30.19-end
Matthew 14.13-end

Tuesday 12 December

Matthew 14.13-end

'We have nothing here but ...' (v.17)

The disciples have some bread and fish, hardly enough to feed themselves after a long day, let alone in excess of 5,000 people. Later, on the lake, they have only fear – fear exacerbated by the sight of a mysterious figure gliding over the waters. The crowds in Gennesaret have little chance of the personal attention Jesus usually gave to those he healed, but they are in such need.

To the disciples who have something in their hands, he tells them to bring what they have to him. Taking that into his hands, he multiplies it. To the disciples in the storm who have nothing in their hearts but fear, he walks towards them, speaking words of peace, transforming their fear into faith. 'Come', he says to Peter, but when Peter's faith fails, he reaches out to save him and lifts the sinking man to safety. To the crowds in Gennesaret, the sick and suffering, so many people in need, pleading with unrealistic expectations, Jesus – as it were – extends himself, and the apparently impossible becomes the actually happening as they touch even the edges of his clothing and are healed.

To those who come to Jesus in every age and every state, he poses the challenge of whether we will rely only on the evidence of our senses, or whether we will trust that his heart truly goes out to us, broken open by the compassion of God for his world, the God whose power is made perfect in our weakness (2 Corinthians 12.9).

Almighty God,
purify our hearts and minds,
that when your Son Jesus Christ comes again as
judge and saviour
we may be ready to receive him,
who is our Lord and our God.

COLLECT

Reflection by **Christopher Cocksworth**

23

Wednesday 13 December

Matthew 15.1-20

'For out of the heart ...' (v.19)

Jesus' public ministry in Galilee is drawing to a close. The shadow of the long walk to Jerusalem begins to loom. Pharisees and scribes travel north from Jerusalem's seat of authority to interrogate Jesus. Perhaps they expect that this rural rabbi, with no credentials, will be put easily into his place. Not a bit of it. For their criticism of his disciples breaking the tradition of the elders, Jesus charges them with breaking the commandments of God and making void the word of the Lord.

Tensions with the religious establishment are escalating, and Jesus, far from easing them, raises them even higher. He gathers a crowd and implores them to understand that a fundamental principle of God's ways is at stake, a principle undermined by the philosophy and practice of scribal orthodoxy. The heart – that driving seat of human attitude and action – is the defining source of personal purity before the personal God. It is with all the strength of the heart that we are to love the Lord our God. Observance of diet and avoidance of dirt without the obedience of the heart will not protect us from defilement. Keeping our hearts close to God determines our capacity to fulfil his law.

Jesus has made a decisive break with his religious culture, a step that sets him on an unstoppable course to Jerusalem, where the obedience of his heart, and the willing offering of his body, creates in us a clean heart and a steadfast spirit (Psalm 51.10). When 'the secrets of the heart' are disclosed, we know that the Christ who comes to the world is at work, and that 'God is really among us' (1 Corinthians 14.24).

COLLECT

O Lord, raise up, we pray, your power
and come among us,
and with great might succour us;
that whereas, through our sins and wickedness
we are grievously hindered
in running the race that is set before us,
your bountiful grace and mercy
may speedily help and deliver us;
through Jesus Christ your Son our Lord,
to whom with you and the Holy Spirit,
be honour and glory, now and for ever.

24 | *Reflection by* **Christopher Cocksworth**

Psalms 53, **54**, 60 *or* **37***
Isaiah 32
Matthew 15.21-28

Thursday 14 December

Matthew 15.21-28

'Lord, help me' (v.25)

It's very interesting the way two treasured pieces from the Communion Service come from the mouths of gentiles who turn to Jesus, Israel's Messiah, for help and healing. Inspired by the centurion (Matthew 8.5-13), we say in our own day, 'Lord, I am not worthy to receive you, but only say the word, and I shall be healed'. Or, drawing on the words of the Canaanite woman in this story, we admit that 'we are not worthy to gather up the crumbs' under the table of the Lord, but we affirm that the Lord's nature is 'always to have mercy'. Both liturgical gems combine humility before God with a confidence in the abundance of divine grace for all, outsiders as we were and sinners as we are.

Jesus' encounter with the woman doesn't make for easy reading. His words seem unusually harsh. Perhaps the baldness of the words on a page hides a gesture of the arm, a twinkle of an eye, a tongue in a cheek. Or perhaps Jesus made his words hard so as to test the faith of the woman, to see whether she really understood that the grace of Israel's God abounded for the gentiles as well.

What is clear is that Jesus had already prophesied that many will come from 'east and west' (Matthew 8.11) and that now, when this woman comes from the west and says, 'Lord, help me', he does as she asks, gladly sharing the bread of healing. She is, indeed, sent away, but not before she – like us today – has been fed with manna that comes down from heaven.

Almighty God,
purify our hearts and minds,
that when your Son Jesus Christ comes again as
judge and saviour
we may be ready to receive him,
who is our Lord and our God.

COLLECT

Reflection by **Christopher Cocksworth** | 25

Friday 15 December

Psalms 85, **86** *or* 31
Isaiah 33.1-22
Matthew 15.29-end

Matthew 15.29-end

'I do not want to send them away hungry' (v.32)

Having headed west towards Tyre, Jesus turned towards the east, probably the gentile region of Decapolis. Walking clockwise around the Sea of Galilee, Jesus climbed into the Golan Heights, perhaps seeking – as he often did – quiet and solitude for prayer. The gentiles, as the Jews before, did not allow that space for himself and God. They came, searching him out in large numbers, bringing with them the sick and suffering, pressing upon him, jostling for their space, hoping for their share in the God of Israel's power.

Jesus did not disappoint them. He healed with the same extravagance as he had done in Jewish circles. Neither, though, did the gentiles disappoint Jesus. Putting their faith in and offering their praise to the God of Israel, they also stayed for a few days with Jesus in the dangerous terrain of the mountains, even to the point of physical risk.

Jesus' heart goes out to them with the same compassion he had for the Jewish crowds who had come to him hungering for healing and hope, yearning for the bread of heaven. But this time the disciples don't even offer the small amount of food they have between them. Jesus may have healed some Gentiles, surely he is not going to miraculously multiply bread for them as well? Had they not understood that 'many will come from east and west and will eat with Abraham, Isaac and Jacob in the kingdom of heaven' (Matthew 8.11)? Have we grasped that Israel's God, and his Messiah, does not want to send any away hungry? Do we live as those who truly believe that God's Son was born the Saviour for all, and that he 'will appear a second time ... to save those who are eagerly waiting for him' (Hebrews 9.28)?

COLLECT

O Lord, raise up, we pray, your power
and come among us,
and with great might succour us;
that whereas, through our sins and wickedness
we are grievously hindered
in running the race that is set before us,
your bountiful grace and mercy
may speedily help and deliver us;
through Jesus Christ your Son our Lord,
to whom with you and the Holy Spirit,
be honour and glory, now and for ever.

26 | *Reflection by* **Christopher Cocksworth**

Psalm **145** *or* 41, **42**, 43
Isaiah 35
Matthew 16.1-12

Saturday 16 December

Matthew 16.1-12

'How could you fail to perceive that I was not speaking about bread?' (v.11)

Here we go again. Religious authorities arrive from Jerusalem to test Jesus, demanding a sign from heaven to give unambiguous authentication of his claims and teaching that caused them so much concern. But as Jesus had earlier told the local leaders, the only sign that will be given, will be the sign of Jonah – the sign of death and resurrection, and even that may fail to convince.

Jesus' exasperation with the Pharisees and Sadducees spills over into an argument with the disciples. How could they be worried about running out of bread? They had seen with their eyes the extraordinary powers at work through him in the feedings of multitudes. Have they not perceived with their hearts the meaning of the miracles? Have they swallowed the toxic leaven of the leaders' cynicism and, despite everything they had seen and heard, still failed to recognize that here, in Jesus, was Israel's Messiah, the Lord's Servant, the Son of Man – the Bread of Life that comes down from heaven to feed the world?

Jesus heads toward the north, far from Jerusalem, and there, he will become the examiner, testing his disciples to see whether he can tease from them the sort of spiritual perception that they will need if they are to stand any chance of bearing the load that will come their way when they walk towards Jerusalem.

Will they finally confess that he is the Messiah, the Son of the living God; and will they take up their cross and follow him? Will we?

Almighty God,
purify our hearts and minds,
that when your Son Jesus Christ comes again as
judge and saviour
we may be ready to receive him,
who is our Lord and our God.

COLLECT

Reflection by **Christopher Cocksworth**

Monday 18 December

Psalm **40** *or* **44**
Isaiah 38. 1-8, 21-22
Matthew 16.13-end

Matthew 16.13-end

'... on this rock' (v.18)

Poor Peter! One minute he's blessed and exalted, and the next he's Satan! One minute he's had a great insight; the next he's made an elementary mistake. Yet right in the middle of this alternation (and altercation!) Peter receives a new name – he becomes 'The Rock', the rock that will be a foundation for others; the rock against which hell shall not prevail. And Jesus is as good as his word: in all Peter's ups and downs, insights and idiocies, affirmations and denials, the one thing that is never in doubt is Christ's rock-solid love for Peter, calling, provoking, almost teasing out his love in return.

And it's the same with us. It's not just that we sometimes have to go from plaudits to brickbats and back again in the blink of an eye – you get used to it, people behave like that. The hardest thing is when it feels as if the Lord himself is wavering – when one day we feel so close, and the next it seems that God is, as the poet Geoffrey Hill said, 'distant, difficult'. That's the Petrine experience. But there's another side to it, as Peter himself discovered. Deep down underneath the current crisis is the Love who is himself our rock and our refuge. Jesus loved Peter even as he fell and loved him into recovery. And in the end it was, as always, the risen Jesus, who set things right – and steadied the rock.

COLLECT

O Lord Jesus Christ,
who at your first coming sent your messenger
to prepare your way before you:
grant that the ministers and stewards of your mysteries
may likewise so prepare and make ready your way
by turning the hearts of the disobedient to the wisdom of the just,
that at your second coming to judge the world
we may be found an acceptable people in your sight;
for you are alive and reign with the Father
in the unity of the Holy Spirit,
one God, now and for ever.

Reflection by **Malcolm Guite**

Psalms 144, **146**
Isaiah 38. 9-20
Matthew 17.1-13

Tuesday 19 December

Matthew 17.1-13

'... he was transfigured before them' (v.2)

I once heard this account of the transfiguration described as 'a misplaced resurrection narrative', as though St Matthew had made a slight error with his laptop's cut and paste feature! There is a real and mysterious way this story is a 'resurrection narrative', but it is certainly not 'misplaced'! As we saw yesterday, Peter had already discerned that Jesus was the true messiah. He had some inkling of Christ's glory, but had no idea what that would mean, or how it must lead to the cross. Now Jesus is turning his face towards Jerusalem, and if his disciples are to sustain the sorrow that awaits them all there, they need this mountaintop moment to sustain them, this glimpse of the true glory, of the joy of the kingdom, the light of the resurrection. The light of mount Tabor is there to accompany them through the darkness and eclipse of Good Friday, and it is indeed a resurrection light, a premonition of Easter dawn. My sonnet on the transfiguration is set on Good Friday and voiced for Peter:

> *A sudden blaze of long-extinguished hope*
> *Trembled and tingled through the tender skin.*
> *Nor can this this blackened sky, this darkened scar,*
> *Eclipse that glimpse of how things really are.**

Maybe it is also good for us, and no 'misplaced narrative', to visit this scene in the dark days of December, days before the light and glory will be veiled in the flesh of the baby at Bethlehem.

*Malcolm Guite, *Sounding the Seasons*, Canterbury Press 2012

Reflection by **Malcolm Guite**   29

Wednesday 20 December

Matthew 17.14-21

'How much longer ...?' (v.17)

'How much longer must I put up with you?' It is at once shocking and comforting to hear these words on the lips of Jesus. Shocking because we have constructed such a safe and sanitized idea of his perfection that we assume that a sinless person would never be exasperated – or at least never give voice to their exasperation. Yet here is Jesus, perfect God and perfect man, utterly exasperated by his own disciples and letting them know! The experience of having delegated a task, only to find it hasn't been done and you have to do it yourself after all is almost universal, so it's good to know that God has been through it too. And here is the comfort: perhaps we needn't be so hard on ourselves when patience wears thin and we sometimes lose our cool, and think – or even say, as Jesus did: 'How much longer must I put up with you?'

But there is more of course, and, as with so many stories of Jesus, a twist in the tail. Jesus may lose *patience* with the disciples and with us, but he never loses *faith*. He turns to them and to us and says: 'Don't ask for more faith; the faith you already have, however tiny it may be, is already more than enough, provided you understand that it is not a strength, or an achievement, it is a seed; not something to hold on to for yourselves, but something to give away so that it grows elsewhere.'

COLLECT

O Lord Jesus Christ,
who at your first coming sent your messenger
to prepare your way before you:
grant that the ministers and stewards of your mysteries
may likewise so prepare and make ready your way
by turning the hearts of the disobedient to the wisdom of the just,
that at your second coming to judge the world
we may be found an acceptable people in your sight;
for you are alive and reign with the Father
in the unity of the Holy Spirit,
one God, now and for ever.

Reflection by **Malcolm Guite**

Thursday 21 December

Matthew 17.22-end

'... cast a hook' (v.27)

I love this story. It's so improper. In the midst of a solemn discussion of tax and tribute, of the mixture of necessity and oppression that goes into funding religion, suddenly comes this magical tale; a tale that feels like it's come from folklore and fairyland; a tale that's full of sheer, delightful, creative serendipity. The context is sombre, indeed, sinister: 'Does your teacher not pay the temple tax?' That is a loaded question! We have just heard Jesus say that he is going to be betrayed. The authorities are looking for any hook they can use to reel Jesus in, and failure to pay a controversial tax might just be the one. After all they try the same ruse again in the temple with the question about Ceasar, which Jesus also answers with a coin.

Here Jesus does something wonderful. In the distinction between children and subjects, he not only affirms what Paul later called 'the glorious liberty of the children of God' (Romans 8.21, KJV), but he also discloses the heart of the gospel: that we are not God's oppressed subjects but his beloved children. However, having established the point in principle, Jesus graciously concedes to paying the tax, so as not to cause unnecessary offence over a small thing (if only his followers also avoided giving unnecessary offence!). And then, with his wonderful searching irony and humour, Jesus suggests that Peter should drop a hook into the sea and reel in something to satisfy those who had hoped to hook and reel him in instead.

God for whom we watch and wait,
you sent John the Baptist to prepare the way of your Son:
give us courage to speak the truth,
to hunger for justice,
and to suffer for the cause of right,
with Jesus Christ our Lord.

COLLECT

Reflection by **Malcolm Guite**   31

Friday 22 December

Matthew 18.1-20

'Who is the greatest ...?' (v.1)

There is so much that is rich and challenging in this reading, but perhaps in these days before Christmas, it is this powerful image of the child in the midst that most calls and draws us. It is the worldly desire amongst the disciples to be 'the greatest' that leads Jesus to place in their midst 'the least', not only the smallest in stature but one of the least regarded, most marginalized, most powerless group in that culture: a child.

Jesus then begins another of his great and creative reversals. He calls the grown-ups to learn a lesson from the children; calls the disciples to change and become child-like again. It is no small thing he is asking: that humility, that willing self-diminishment, setting aside power and privilege, refusing to tower over people. But Jesus never asks of us anything he does not do himself. We read this story on the brink of Christmas, approaching the day when we remember that the king of heaven himself did indeed change and become like a little child – indeed more than just *like* a child, for the God of heaven came down and became a child, that he might find, redeem and enthrone the child in us, and that we in turn might welcome, and find our welcome in, the lowest and the least, rather than wasting our breath on the heart-withering question: 'Who is the greatest?'

COLLECT

O Lord Jesus Christ,
who at your first coming sent your messenger
to prepare your way before you:
grant that the ministers and stewards of your mysteries
may likewise so prepare and make ready your way
by turning the hearts of the disobedient to the wisdom of the just,
that at your second coming to judge the world
we may be found an acceptable people in your sight;
for you are alive and reign with the Father
in the unity of the Holy Spirit,
one God, now and for ever.

Reflection by **Malcolm Guite**

Saturday 23 December

Matthew 18.21-end

'... seventy-seven times' (v.22)

C. S. Lewis has a nice take on this call to forgive 77 times. He says it may not be that we have to forgive 77 separate offences; it's that it may take us 77 attempts to forgive someone fully even once. We forgive them. We say 'I've let it go'. Then that night we remember the offence again. It rankles. We get cross. We suddenly realize we haven't really forgiven them, so we sigh and forgive again, saying 'Now that's done'. But then, something else reminds us and we have to start again. We may only have said 'I forgive' out loud once, but there's been a lot more unspoken forgiving to do.

If that is so, if it is so hard to forgive, if we find ourselves trapped in a repetitive loop of resentment, then Jesus' outrageous parable of the two debtors might reframe everything for us and break the cycle. In this story we are invited to give up playing the tiresome role of the magnanimous (but secretly resentful) forgiver and suddenly remember that we are also the unexpectedly, utterly, forgiven. Then, instead of the effort to muster up a feeling we may not have, we can let sheer gratitude for our own undeserved release from guilt flow out naturally into release and peace for others.

God for whom we watch and wait,
you sent John the Baptist to prepare the way of your Son:
give us courage to speak the truth,
to hunger for justice,
and to suffer for the cause of right,
with Jesus Christ our Lord.

COLLECT

Morning Prayer – a simple form

O Lord, open our lips
and our mouth shall proclaim your praise.

A prayer of thanksgiving for Advent

Blessed are you, Sovereign God of all,
to you be praise and glory for ever.
In your tender compassion
the dawn from on high is breaking upon us
to dispel the lingering shadows of night.
As we look for your coming among us this day,
open our eyes to behold your presence
and strengthen our hands to do your will,
that the world may rejoice and give you praise.
Blessed be God, Father, Son and Holy Spirit.
Blessed be God for ever.

Word of God

Psalmody *(the psalm or psalms listed for the day)*

**Glory to the Father and to the Son
and to the Holy Spirit;
as it was in the beginning is now:
and shall be for ever. Amen.**

Reading from Holy Scripture *(one or both of the passages set for the day)*

Reflection

The Benedictus (The Song of Zechariah) *(see opposite page)*

Prayers

Intercessions – a time of prayer for the day and its tasks, the world and its need, the church and her life.

The Collect for the Day

The Lord's Prayer *(see p. 37)*

Conclusion

A blessing or the Grace *(see p. 37)*, or a concluding response

Let us bless the Lord
Thanks be to God

Benedictus (The Song of Zechariah)

1 Blessed be the Lord the God of Israel, ◆
   who has come to his people and set them free.

2 He has raised up for us a mighty Saviour, ◆
   born of the house of his servant David.

3 Through his holy prophets God promised of old ◆
   to save us from our enemies,
      from the hands of all that hate us,

4 To show mercy to our ancestors, ◆
   and to remember his holy covenant.

5 This was the oath God swore to our father Abraham: ◆
   to set us free from the hands of our enemies,

6 Free to worship him without fear, ◆
   holy and righteous in his sight
      all the days of our life.

7 And you, child, shall be called the prophet of the Most High, ◆
   for you will go before the Lord to prepare his way,

8 To give his people knowledge of salvation ◆
   by the forgiveness of all their sins.

9 In the tender compassion of our God ◆
   the dawn from on high shall break upon us,

10 To shine on those who dwell in darkness
      and the shadow of death, ◆
   and to guide our feet into the way of peace.

Luke 1.68-79

**Glory to the Father and to the Son
and to the Holy Spirit;
as it was in the beginning is now:
and shall be for ever. Amen.**

Seasonal Prayers of Thanksgiving

Advent

Blessed are you, Sovereign God of all,
to you be praise and glory for ever.
In your tender compassion
the dawn from on high is breaking upon us
to dispel the lingering shadows of night.
As we look for your coming among us this day,
open our eyes to behold your presence
and strengthen our hands to do your will,
that the world may rejoice and give you praise.
Blessed be God, Father, Son and Holy Spirit.
Blessed be God for ever.

At Any Time

Blessed are you, creator of all,
to you be praise and glory for ever.
As your dawn renews the face of the earth
bringing light and life to all creation,
may we rejoice in this day you have made;
as we wake refreshed from the depths of sleep,
open our eyes to behold your presence
and strengthen our hands to do your will,
that the world may rejoice and give you praise.
Blessed be God, Father, Son and Holy Spirit.
Blessed be God for ever.

after Lancelot Andrewes (1626)

The Lord's Prayer and The Grace

Our Father in heaven,
hallowed be your name,
your kingdom come,
your will be done,
on earth as in heaven.
Give us today our daily bread.
Forgive us our sins
as we forgive those who sin against us.
Lead us not into temptation
but deliver us from evil.
For the kingdom, the power,
and the glory are yours
now and for ever.
Amen.

(or)

Our Father, who art in heaven,
hallowed be thy name;
thy kingdom come;
thy will be done;
on earth as it is in heaven.
Give us this day our daily bread.
And forgive us our trespasses,
as we forgive those who trespass against us.
And lead us not into temptation;
but deliver us from evil.
For thine is the kingdom,
the power and the glory,
for ever and ever.
Amen.

The grace of our Lord Jesus Christ,
and the love of God,
and the fellowship of the Holy Spirit,
be with us all evermore.
Amen.

An Order for Night Prayer (Compline)

Preparation

The Lord almighty grant us a quiet night and a perfect end.
Amen.

Our help is in the name of the Lord
who made heaven and earth.

A period of silence for reflection on the past day may follow.

The following or other suitable words of penitence may be used

Most merciful God,
we confess to you,
before the whole company of heaven and one another,
that we have sinned in thought, word and deed
and in what we have failed to do.
Forgive us our sins,
heal us by your Spirit
and raise us to new life in Christ. Amen.

O God, make speed to save us.
O Lord, make haste to help us.

Glory to the Father and to the Son
and to the Holy Spirit;
as it was in the beginning is now
and shall be for ever. Amen.
Alleluia.

The following or another suitable hymn may be sung

Before the ending of the day,
Creator of the world, we pray
That you, with steadfast love, would keep
Your watch around us while we sleep.

From evil dreams defend our sight,
From fears and terrors of the night;
Tread underfoot our deadly foe
That we no sinful thought may know.

O Father, that we ask be done
Through Jesus Christ, your only Son;
And Holy Spirit, by whose breath
Our souls are raised to life from death.

The Word of God

One or more of Psalms 4, 91 or 134 may be used.

Psalm 134

1   Come, bless the Lord, all you servants of the Lord, ♦
    you that by night stand in the house of the Lord.

2   Lift up your hands towards the sanctuary ♦
    and bless the Lord.

3   The Lord who made heaven and earth ♦
    give you blessing out of Zion.

**Glory to the Father and to the Son
and to the Holy Spirit;
as it was in the beginning is now
and shall be for ever. Amen.**

Scripture Reading

*One of the following short lessons or another suitable
passage is read*

You, O Lord, are in the midst of us and we are called by your
name; leave us not, O Lord our God.

Jeremiah 14.9

(or)

Be sober, be vigilant, because your adversary the devil is
prowling round like a roaring lion, seeking for someone
to devour. Resist him, strong in the faith.

1 Peter 5.8,9

(or)

The servants of the Lamb shall see the face of God, whose name
will be on their foreheads. There will be no more night: they will
not need the light of a lamp or the light of the sun, for God will
be their light, and they will reign for ever and ever.

Revelation 22.4,5

Into your hands, O Lord, I commend my spirit.
Into your hands, O Lord, I commend my spirit.
For you have redeemed me, Lord God of truth.
I commend my spirit.
Glory to the Father and to the Son
and to the Holy Spirit.
Into your hands, O Lord, I commend my spirit.

Or, in Easter

Into your hands, O Lord, I commend my spirit.
Alleluia, alleluia.
Into your hands, O Lord, I commend my spirit.
Alleluia, alleluia.
For you have redeemed me, Lord God of truth.
Alleluia, alleluia.
Glory to the Father and to the Son
and to the Holy Spirit.
Into your hands, O Lord, I commend my spirit.
Alleluia, alleluia.

Keep me as the apple of your eye.
Hide me under the shadow of your wings.

Gospel Canticle

Nunc Dimittis (The Song of Simeon)

Save us, O Lord, while waking,
and guard us while sleeping,
that awake we may watch with Christ
and asleep may rest in peace.

1   Now, Lord, you let your servant go in peace:
    your word has been fulfilled.

2   My own eyes have seen the salvation
    which you have prepared in the sight of every people;

3   A light to reveal you to the nations
    and the glory of your people Israel.

Luke 2.29-32

40

Glory to the Father and to the Son
and to the Holy Spirit;
as it was in the beginning is now
and shall be for ever. Amen.

Save us, O Lord, while waking,
and guard us while sleeping,
that awake we may watch with Christ
and asleep may rest in peace.

Prayers

Intercessions and thanksgivings may be offered here.

The Collect

Visit this place, O Lord, we pray,
and drive far from it the snares of the enemy;
may your holy angels dwell with us and guard us in peace,
and may your blessing be always upon us;
through Jesus Christ our Lord.
Amen.

The Lord's Prayer (see p. 37) may be said.

The Conclusion

In peace we will lie down and sleep;
for you alone, Lord, make us dwell in safety.

Abide with us, Lord Jesus,
for the night is at hand and the day is now past.

As the night watch looks for the morning,
so do we look for you, O Christ.

[Come with the dawning of the day
and make yourself known in the breaking of the bread.]

The Lord bless us and watch over us;
the Lord make his face shine upon us and be gracious to us;
the Lord look kindly on us and give us peace.
Amen.

Love what you've read?

Why not consider using *Reflections for Daily Prayer* all year round? We also publish these Bible reflections in an annual format, containing material for the entire church year.

The volume for the **2017/18** church year is now available and features contributions from a host of distinguished writers: Christopher Cocksworth, Gillian Cooper, Stephen Cottrell, Steven Croft, Maggi Dawn, Malcolm Guite, Christopher Herbert, John Kiddle, Barbara Mosse, Mark Oakley, Martyn Percy, John Pritchard, Ben Quash, Angela Tilby, Catherine Williams, Jane Williams, Lucy Winkett, Christopher Woods and Jeremy Worthen.

REFLECTIONS FOR DAILY PRAYER
Advent 2017 to the eve of Advent 2018
ISBN 978 1 78140 019 7 • £16.99

Please note: this book reproduces the material for Advent found in the volume you are now holding.

Reflections for Daily Prayer **2018/19** will be available from May 2018 with reflections written by: Justine Allain Chapman, Kate Bruce, Steven Croft, Paula Gooder, Peter Graystone, Helen-Ann Hartley, David Hoyle, Graham James, Jan McFarlane, Libby Lane, Gordon Mursell, Helen Orchard, John Perumbalath, David Runcorn, Sarah Rowland Jones, Harry Steele, Richard Sudworth, Angela Tilby, Graham Tomlin and Margaret Whipp.

REFLECTIONS FOR DAILY PRAYER
Advent 2018 to the eve of Advent 2019
ISBN 978 1 78140 007 4   £16.99 • 336 pages

REFLECTIONS FOR DAILY PRAYER
App

Make Bible study and reflection a part of your routine wherever you go with the Reflections for Daily Prayer App for Apple and Android devices.

Download the app for free from the App Store (Apple devices) or Google Play (Android devices) and receive a week's worth of reflections free. Then purchase a monthly, three-monthly or annual subscription to receive up-to-date content.

REFLECTIONS FOR SUNDAYS

Reflections for Sundays offers over 250 reflections on the Principal Readings for every Sunday and major Holy Day in Year B, from the same experienced team of writers that have made *Reflections for Daily Prayer* so successful. For each Sunday and major Holy Day, they provide:

- full lectionary details for the Principal Service
- a reflection on each Old Testament reading (both Continuous and Related)
- a reflection on the Epistle
- a reflection on the Gospel.

This book also contains a substantial introduction to the Gospels of Mark and John, written by Paula Gooder.

£14.99 • 288 pages
ISBN 978 1 78140 030 2

Also available in Kindle and epub formats

REFLECTIONS ON THE PSALMS

£14.99 • 192 pages
ISBN 978 0 7151 4490 9

Reflections on the Psalms provides original and insightful meditations on each of the Bible's 150 Psalms.

Each reflection is accompanied by its corresponding Psalm refrain and prayer from the *Common Worship Psalter*, making this a valuable resource for personal or devotional use.

Specially written introductions by Paula Gooder and Steven Croft explore the Psalms and the Bible and the Psalms in the life of the Church.